ISBN 9798548811349

Matters of the Mind
30 Day Devotional
"Transforming Your Thinking"

*Independently Published

Printed in the United States

Matters of the MIND

30 Day Devotional
Transforming Your Thinking

Nikilya Brown McNeil

Introduction

James 1:12 ESV declares, "Blessed is the man who remains steadfast under trial, for when he has stood the test he will receive the crown of life, which God has promised to those who love Him.

Funny how I have discovered the true meaning of myself in this very scripture. Have you ever found yourself stuck in your own thinking? The place where your thoughts led you down paths of pain and destruction? Waking up wondering if life would soon be over, or would you have to continue facing the anguish of another day, another minute or even the pressure of a simple second? I can honestly say I have been there. After battling years of depression that started from the mere thought that I never belonged here, I found myself adding the unhealthy pattern of negative thinking to what was already a danger zone to mental health. Because no one around me understood the level of danger I was in, it took nearly 30 years to receive the help needed to break free of the mental state that tried to destroy me. A mind full of clutter and thoughts of overflowing mess was all a part of my everyday living until I decided to put a stop to it.

Never would I have imagined the day would come when my mind was no longer bound by the abundant thoughts of negativism. It took determination to arrive at this place. I was steadfast at freeing my mind by all means necessary. Over three years ago, I decided to take a little journey-one that would provide me the needed freedom I deserved in order to live a healthy and longer life. This journey was the freedom walk to clear the matters of my own mind. No longer would I accept that being bound by my thoughts would be my new normal.

Something had to give, and I decided to take it by force. This was not an easy process, but every fight for freedom has been well worth it. I woke up daily asking God to speak to me in ways I would understand His plan for providing me with a better way of thinking. In this 30-Day

Devotional, I would like to take you on a mental journey to obtain better thinking. This devotional is a glimpse of the type of thinking that led me to mental freedom. Allowing me to shine light on what was once a dark situation is the purpose of this God-given assignment.

Waking up free from thoughts of regret, unworthiness, disappointment, disgustion and so much more has been one of the greatest blessings God provided me. I dare not refrain from sharing a plan that has the power to change your entire mental being. I want to see you mentally free because your best life is one that is led by the ability to see beyond your thoughts. Take this journey to deal with the matters of your mind by becoming determined to transform your thinking.

Day 1

There is nothing more important than being mentally free. Will you forget all the hurtful things that ever happened to you...of course not! It's senseless to hold on to the false reality of thinking you will never experience the memory of a bad thought. One of the best and most effective ways to deal with those thoughts that once caused so much pain is to turn them into tools utilized to operate on purpose. Everything you have ever gone through has reason attached to it. Remember the saying "what doesn't kill you makes you stronger"? Now it is time to discover the strength in what felt like death. God's desire for your life isn't to cause a continual mental burden. Ask Him to guide your thinking as you trust His plan to lead you in how you should deal with your thoughts.

Scripture: Exodus 15:12 NIV

The Lord is my strength and my defense: He has become my salvation. He is my God, and I will praise Him, my father's God, and I will exalt Him.

Day 2

What we think of ourselves should be in alignment with the thoughts God has toward us. We are created in the image of Christ. Remember God never made anything He deemed as a mess. According to Genesis 1:31, God looked over all He had made and He saw it was good. Stop viewing yourself as a failure or a disgrace to God. Since everything He made was good, remind yourself that you are a part of His everything.

Scripture: Romans 12:2 NLT

Don't copy the behavior and customs of this world, but let God transform you into a new person by changing the way you think. Then you will learn to know God's will for you, which is good, pleasing and perfect.

Day 3

If you are expected to build your hope, why would you leave your thoughts behind? Thoughts shouldn't be left constantly unattended to, or shall I say not dealt with. Your thoughts are like little children in a sense. You wouldn't leave them alone to tend to themselves without providing proper instructions because you don't know what they will find themselves getting into. Children come up with ways to entertain themselves and so do your thoughts when left with too much idle time. It is extremely important to maintain your thoughts as you work toward the process of building your hope and faith to think better. The three feed off of each other. It's time to work on building a mental manual meant to provide instructions on how to execute better thinking.

Scripture: 2 Corinthians 4:17-18 NIV

For our light and momentary troubles are achieving for us an eternal glory that far outweighs them all. So we fix our eyes not on what is seen, but on what is unseen, since what is seen is temporary, but what is unseen is eternal.

Day 4

Ask yourself why you feel the way you do toward certain people and certain things. How did you become so bitter or numb? You want to love them, but struggle with doing so. You want to trust them but can't let your guard down. You know you should forgive them, but every time you try, a flutter seems to take over in your heart to stop you. All of these feelings are led by overwhelming thoughts of what happened to you, and they're hindering "*you*" from moving past them. Remember, the mind tells the heart what to do. If your mind will never let your heart heal, how do you think you'll move ahead to your healed self? Get your mind in line so your heart will follow.

Scripture: Psalm 51:10 AMP

Create in me a clean heart O God, and renew the right and steadfast spirit within me

Day 5

How can God fill you with wisdom and knowledge if negativity and hurt continues to take up necessary space in your mind? It is time to do some house cleaning. This house isn't one that comes fully furnished with material things. This one holds all your other goods. Get rid of every thought that holds no purpose to building a better and stronger "*you*". If the thoughts fail to bring about good, get rid of them.

Scripture: Philippians 4:8 NLT

And now dear brothers and sisters, one final thing. Fix your thoughts on what is true, and honorable, and right, and pure, and lovely, and admirable. Think about things that are excellent and worthy of praise.

Day 6

You can control the thoughts you harbor in your mind. Who says you have to hold on to every memory of hurt that caused you pain and have held you mentally hostage? As a wise woman once said, "It is important to command your thoughts." (Cindy Trimm) Order your thoughts to get in line with God's plan for your life that He vowed would cause you no harm. If what you constantly think about causes unnecessary weight, command the thoughts to be removed by the power and authority of God granted to you. You have the power to command departure of what does not have the right to remain. Walk in your God-given authority to control what is trying to control you.

Scripture: 2 Corinthians 10:5 ESV

We destroy arguments and every lofty opinion raised against the knowledge of God, and take every thought captive to obey Christ.

Day 7

Change the way you think of painful situations you encountered or are currently experiencing in life. Oftentimes, we view our hardest attacks as those that come to devour us. What we view as most powerful to devour will be the very thing God chooses to use in order to launch you into a greater and stronger connection to Him. There is no argument that the situation(s) isn't painful, but God has the ability to give your pain a well-served purpose. View those situations as a part of your "ALL THINGS". Know that it is necessary to have the thoughts of some tragic situations to work together with the thoughts of your triumphs.

Scripture: Romans 8:28 KJV

And we know that all things work together for good to them that love God, to them who are called according to His purpose.

Day 8

You continue to think you have to remember how bad you were hurt or how often you messed up so you will not make the same mistake again. What happened to your faith in God? Isn't He a Protector and Guide? You do not have to keep replaying the pain to keep yourself from traveling that path again. Simply trust God as your Guide and the one who has the ability to protect you from all harm-even the harm you have caused yourself. God is a keeper of your thoughts if you give Him the permission to take the lead in your thinking.

Scripture: Psalm 121:5 KJV

The Lord is the Keeper: the Lord is thy shade upon the right hand.

Day 9

God had no plans to cause you misery. Understand that life happens, and during that time, things can become a bit complicated. While trying to find your way, different mental weights discover ways to attach themselves to your mind. This happens because a lot of times, we spend so much time trying to figure out the *why* and *what* concerning our lives. Because we can't see the details of our story line, we begin to blame God for allowing us to become so miserable. It is time we flip this. Think of those things as a benefit to get you to where you need to go in life. There is no need to continue being angry with God for what He didn't allow to destroy you. No more wasting that level of energy. Focus on God being with you in order to help you through every obstacle ahead. Let Him be your guide and not your punching bag. He doesn't deserve the blame of what was never intended to harm you.

Scripture: John 14:27 ESV

Peace I leave with you; my peace I give to you. Not as the world gives do I give to you. Let not your hearts be troubled, neither let them be afraid.

Day 10

If I say the process of better thinking is easy, I would be lying to you. One of the biggest attacks you will ever experience will be the constant attack of your mind. You won't hear me saying the process is easy, but I will always advocate it is worth it. Releasing what came to take your sanity is painful because it is rooted in the depth of your brain. It will take some digging to get the core of the issue out. You have to work on removing the root that caused the damage. Removing the root will be a painful process, but a purposeful one.

Scripture: Ephesians 4:23-24 AMP

And be continually renewed in the spirit of your mind having a fresh, untarnished mental and spiritual attitude, and put on the new self (the regenerated and renewed nature), created in

God's image (God like) in the righteousness and
holiness of the truth (living in a way that
expresses to God your gratitude for your
salvation).

Day 11

The darkness from your past isn't worth stealing the peace and light of your present and future. Bad things happened, but the good thing is none of it destroyed you. Instead of continuing to think on those things that were not a part of your best, focus on what matters most. Ultimately, it's a matter of who matters most, and that is you. Stop crying over things of your past. Instead, become determined enough to build from it. Every trying time came with a lesson. Leave the thoughts of darkness behind you. It's time to move toward the brighter journey of your life.

Scripture: Isaiah: 9:2 NLT

The people who walk in darkness will see a great light. For those who live in a land of deep darkness, a light will shine.

Day 12

Just when you feel you have overcome the torment that constantly runs rapid in your mind, something happens to remind you of the pain, anger, and/or humiliation the situation caused. This is when you focus on what matters most, and that is knowing God has a plan for your life that is far greater than your problems. Anything other than that really doesn't matter.

Scripture: Jeremiah 29:11 NLT

"For I know the plans I have for you", says the Lord. They are plans for good and not for disaster, to give you a future and a hope.

Day 13

The process of taking control of your thoughts will not be easy. Dealing with the pain from mental burden can be one of the most challenging tasks you will ever face. Keep recalling your reasons for why it is a must you accomplish this. Purpose is a part of God's plan for your healing. God will utilize your survival success to place you before others who need to see proof of His ability to heal and provide a conqueror's mentality. Challenges will be placed in front of you, but you must make up in your mind that none of them deserve the power to derail you from your need for healing. Your reason for creation is attached to getting through this. Although the process is hard, do not give your thoughts the power to say what you can't do.

Scripture: Philippians 4:13 NLT

For I can do all things through Christ, who strengthens me.

Day 14

Distractions will come to stand on the forefront to attempt to derail your plans to obtain better thinking. Don't even think of being defeated. You got this, and there is no devil in hell that can prove to you differently unless you allow it. Refuse to give your way of thinking the ability to stop you. If you push past what is meant to distract you, you will become not only a better person, but a determined individual as well. No negative thought that rises in your mind should be given the power to hinder your process of healing.

Scripture: 2 Chronicles 15:7 NLT

But as for you, be strong and courageous, for your work will be rewarded.

Day 15

There will be days when you feel you haven't made any progress in the betterment of your thinking. Seems as if you are facing the same mental challenges you started the healing process with. Do not allow exhaustion and discouragement to halt what God is doing for you mentally. Remember, every ounce of freedom counts for something. Every step you have taken has gotten you closer to your healing. Keep going as you continue to focus on the greater goal. Ask yourself what exactly is this goal. Let me suggest it is to become a completely healed "*you*".

Scripture: Galatians 6:9 ISV

Let's not get tired of doing what is good, for at the right time we will reap a harvest—if we do not give up.

Day 16

Refuse to allow the thoughts of what happened to you in the past to hinder you from what awaits you in your future. You are not what happened to you, neither are you the failure your mind keeps replaying you are. Allow me to remind you that your past is your past for a reason. There is more in front of you than what you left behind. Regardless of what your thoughts say, you survived that part.

Scripture: Deuteronomy 7:6-8 ESV

It was not because you were more in number than any other people that the LORD set His love on you and chose you, for you were the fewest of all peoples, but it is because the LORD loves you and is keeping the oath that He swore to your fathers, that the LORD has brought you out with a mighty hand and redeemed you from

the house of slavery, from the hand of Pharaoh
king of Egypt.

Day 17

Your thoughts can lead you to some of the most dangerous places-to areas that will cause you the most harm. Feelings of unworthiness, hatred, unforgiveness, regret and so many other areas are to name a few. Some people think the most dangerous place to be is a physical setting, but I stand and argue to differ. The most dangerous place to find yourself is in the middle of wrestling with your thoughts. Negative thinking can keep you in more trouble that you realize. Stop traveling to mental places that cause you harm. Get out of that place and find safety.

Scripture: Romans 8:5 KJV

For they that are after the flesh do mind the things of the flesh; but they that are after the Spirit the things of the Spirit.

Day 18

It is up to you to survive the thoughts of being damaged goods. You would not feel that way if you refuse to think that way. There is a treasure in the most damaged thing. You have to simply discover it and realize the value of what you hold. Not only can this jewel be found in you, but you must also realize that the value and treasure is *"you"*.

Scripture: 2 Corinthians 5:17 KJV

Therefore, if any man be in Christ, he is a new creature: old things are passed away; behold, all things are become new.

Day 19

Deal with it! How many times are you going to say you want to be free from the thoughts that keep causing you so much anguish? Year after year, you find yourself going around this same mental mountain. How tall will you let it become? How big will you allow this beast to grow? Again I say, deal with it! Now is the time you make up your mind to put in the work. I will be the first to say it won't be easy, but it will definitely be worth it. Promise yourself you will not hold back your healing. You owe your mind the freedom. This may be one of your hardest challenges, but a made-up mind can be one of your greatest accomplishments. Keep encouraging yourself that you will make it through this, no matter the challenges placed before you or the obstacles that seem too big to master. Your mental state deserves your best effort to deal with the issues so you can experience freedom and wholeness. You don't have to do this alone. The Holy Spirit is here to assist, but first you must make up your mind you want the help.

Scripture: Proverbs 16:3 NET

Commit your works to the Lord, and your plans will be established.

Day 20

     Sitting and contemplating whether you want to seek help or not isn't helping you. The more time you waste trying to talk your negative thoughts out so others will not notice your struggle, the more time you have lost to obtain necessary help. You know what is troubling you. You know exactly what's resting in your mind trying to block your freedom. As much as you try not to focus on it, the thoughts are still there. It's like ignoring stinky trash as it sits and gains more uncomfortable order because no one wants to take it out. It's time to clean the house. Put down that broom and stop sweeping trash under the rug. Pick up a thought one at a time to clear what doesn't belong. Properly discard it so it will not be placed in areas meant to affect something else. You don't have time to waste. Life is too precious to let trash stay there to stink up your whole life. Get the help you need to rid yourself of unnecessary waste so you can enjoy the fullness of life. Your better days are ahead of you. Think your way to them.

Scripture: Psalm 39:4 NLT

Lord, remind me how brief my time on earth will be. Remind me that my days are numbered-how fleeting my life is. You have made my life no longer than the width of my hand. My entire lifetime is just a moment to you; at best, each of us is but a breath. We are merely moving shadows, and all our busy rushing ends in nothing. We heap up wealth, not knowing who will spend it. And so, Lord, where do I put my hope? My only hope is in You.

Day 21

The thoughts keep playing in your mind because you haven't done the hard part to silence them. You are giving them too much power. Take control now or lose all forms of control later. You run your thoughts, so refuse to let them run you. The power to snatch the volume away from what continues to play loudly in your mind is in your control. Mute what doesn't matter. Ask yourself if remembering it will cause you growth or weaken you as you go. What has the ability to weaken should be stopped in its tracks. If thoughts aren't meant to build, then their only purpose is meant to hinder or kill. Kill may be a strong word to use, but negative thinking has the power to kill every dream, every desire, and every bit of your purpose if you let it fester too long. Tear down every thought that is trying to destroy.

Scripture: 2 Corinthians 10:4-5 KJV

For the weapons of our warfare are not carnal, but mighty through God to the pulling down of strongholds. Casting down imaginations, and every high thing that exalteth itself against the knowledge of God, and bringing into captivity every thought to the obedience of Christ.

Day 22

The ongoing thoughts are so troubling because you have fed them until they have grown in mental power. There used to be a time when painful memories would pass through your mind without stopping; but now, it seems these same memories are your strongest mental entertainment. Why are you allowing something to hang around that is no longer welcomed? These thoughts are your unwanted guests. Kick them out! You constantly pay the cost to be the boss of your own mind. The word of God provides instructions on what to think on. Thoughts of peace, joy, and purpose should be special guests on your mental attendee list. Anything else has no run or right to stay.

Scripture: Philippians 4:7-8 KJV

And the peace of God, which passeth all understanding, shall keep your hearts and minds through Christ Jesus. Finally, brethren, whatsoever things are true, whatsoever things are honest, whatsoever things are just, whatsoever things are pure, whatsoever things are lovely, whatsoever things are of good report; if there be any virtue, and if there be any praise, think on these things.

Day 23

Since God is concerned about our cares, why should we think He will neglect being concerned about our daily thoughts? What we think has the ability to weigh heavier on us than what we do. God has provided instructions on lightening the mental load. Some things carry too much weight. At some point, we must discover how vital it will be to let it go. Negative thinking puts pressure on you. There is no point in weighing yourself down with pressure when you have someone capable of carrying what concerns you. Release the weight to release the pressure. Trade the heaviness of your thinking with the freedom God has made available to you. God has the ability to handle what you can't. He is waiting for you to make the exchange.

Scripture: 1 Peter 5:7-11 NLT

Give all your worries and cares to God, for He cares about you. Stay alert! Watch out for your great enemy, the devil. He prowls around like a roaring lion, looking for someone to devour. Stand firm against him, and be strong in your faith. Remember that your family of believers all over the world is going through the same kind of suffering you are. In His kindness God called you to share in His eternal glory by means of Christ Jesus. So after you have suffered a little while, He will restore, support, and strengthen you, and He will place you on a firm foundation. All power to Him forever! Amen

Day 24

Pressing through the crowd of your thoughts is majorly important. You will have to push through pain to get to the other side. As you maneuver through, you will encounter situations that remind you of the very things that have burdened your mental state of being. The fact that they hurt you, no one ever loved you, you are always alone, or you should not even be here are just bits of the clutter in your head. You have to remember the authority granted to you by God that causes you to trample on the head of the serpent. Those negative thoughts are like snakes. They are sneaky, and carry so much mental poison. I challenge you to step on every thought that tries to raise its evil head against you and your healing.

Scripture: Luke 10:19 KJV

Behold, I give unto you power to tread on serpents and scorpions, and over all the power of the enemy: and nothing shall by any means hurt you.

Day 25

A determined mindset will lead you to areas you never thought you had the ability to see. Negative thinking keeps you away as your thoughts remain in bondage or a place of complacency. Ask yourself whether you want to be guided by negative thinking or led by determination. Regardless of the environment around you, the way you think will determine how long your mind remains there. Do not get stuck in mental bondage that causes a delay in forward movement to a better "you". Wake up your thoughts to wake up the best you.

Scripture: Romans 15:4-6 NASB

For whatever was written in earlier times was written for our instruction, so that through perseverance and the encouragement of the Scriptures we might have hope. Now may the

God who gives perseverance and encouragement grant you to be of the same mind with one another, according to Christ Jesus, so that with one purpose *and* one voice you may glorify the God and Father of our Lord Jesus Christ.

Day 26

Days will come when you want to throw in the towel because you feel you haven't accomplished anything when it comes to your mental state. It will seem like what you are doing isn't working. All of the decrees, declarations, and positive affirmations will seem to have no power and purpose. You may even ask yourself why keep speaking things that hold no truth concerning you. This is the time you choose to go harder for your healing. Satan has recognized you are closer than what you were before determining to break free. Keep speaking positivity all around you. Continue to command alignment concerning your thoughts. Continue to go before God boldly to remind Him of what He has said about your ability to become free. Don't be moved by your feelings. Focus on the future and what is in front of you to gain. You have come too far to quit. Continue to open your mouth to declare what you want to see, how you want to think, and the way you want to feel that aligns with God's word. Wear Satan's plots and plan out! You have the power to do this. Keep believing and decreeing it.

Scripture: Romans 5:1-4 NLT

Therefore, since we have been made right in God's sight by faith, we have peace with God because of what Jesus Christ our Lord has done for us. Because of our faith, Christ has brought us into this place of undeserved privilege where we now stand, and we confidently and joyfully look forward to sharing God's glory. We can rejoice, too, when we run into problems and trials, for we know that they help us develop endurance. And endurance develops strength of character, and character strengthens our confident hope of salvation.

Day 27

The manual will not be at your reach at all times. This is when you must remember what it took to become free. Freedom took you making up in your mind that you refuse to be bound again. Freedom took your determination. It also took your perseverance. Don't get this far and turn around to the old broken "you". Remember the principles you applied in order to break all of the heaviness off your mind. Think about the choices you made to gain or regain your peace. Just because the chain was broken from your thoughts doesn't mean you are in the clear from another lockdown. Remaining free is a process that will need your attention and effort on a daily basis. Satan's job is to break you again. Don't let your mind employ him. Once fired, let him remain in that status. Your job is to maintain your freedom by all means necessary.

Scripture: Galatians 5:1 NKJV

Stand fast therefore in the liberty by which Christ has made us free, and do not be entangled again with a yoke of bondage.

Day 28

Making it to the finish line of mental freedom is no longer on the backburner of your mind. At this point you have made it your conscious choice. You should be proud of yourself. Now that you have decided to put your freedom first, keep this a priority. Do not get this far and turn around to return to your old way of thinking. Keeping what you have fought so hard for is worth the continued work. I understand there will be times when you get tired, but do not quit at being your greatest freedom fighter. Let this form of healing be a race you will always be determined to finish. A successful runner never stops in the middle of the race. They gain their momentum by setting a goal to cross the finish line. As you continue this journey traveling toward a more healed mental state, make sure you always recall what it felt like to cross the finish line. Mental stability is a continued race, so you will experience multiple finishes. Each time you run, remember to leave every thought that tries to negatively attach itself to you behind. If it causes harm, drop it off to its destination and keep moving. God will tell you what to keep and what should be trashed. Nothing that tries to destroy you deserves to finish with you unless it is needed to coach others to their win.

Scripture: Ecclesiastes 9:11 KJV

I returned, and saw under the sun, that the race is not to the swift, nor the battle to the strong, neither yet bread to the wise, nor yet riches to men of understanding, nor yet favour to men of skill; but time and chance happeneth to them all.

Day 29

Never allow the opinions of people to hinder you from maintaining or keeping your mental healing. Some will disagree with your method to heal. This is a problem you don't have to entertain. God will vindicate you from every ill word or tactic they attempted to use to bring shame to your name or character. Instead of putting a halt to the process in order to pamper someone else's ego or emotions, keep seeking God's face on how to continue executing His plan to keep you healed. You have fought with mental struggles long enough. If people don't have the power to heal you, refuse to allow them to hinder you.

Scripture: Isaiah 54:17 ESV

"No weapon that is formed against you will succeed; And every tongue that rises against you in judgment you will condemn. This [peace, righteousness, security, and triumph over opposition] is the heritage of the servants of the Lord, And *this is* their vindication from Me," says the Lord.

Day 30

One of the greatest joys of mental freedom is seeing others benefit from it. Oftentimes, those closest to you battle along with you. Seeing you suffer causes them distress. When you heal for yourself, you also heal others. The more you are released from mental clutter, the lighter the weight becomes for those who love you most. Now that the load is lifted, celebrate with those you love and the ones who love you. This accomplishment deserves the accolades.

Scripture: Psalm 150:1-6 KJV

Praise ye the Lord. Praise God in His sanctuary: praise Him in the firmament of His power. Praise Him for His mighty acts: praise Him according to His excellent greatness. Praise Him with the sound of the trumpet: praise Him with the psaltery and harp. Praise Him with the timbrel and dance: praise Him with stringed instruments and organs. Praise Him upon the loud cymbals: praise Him upon the high sounding cymbals. Let everything that hath breath praise the Lord. Praise ye the Lord.

Prayer

Father, You have been the guide in the path to healing. Thank You for allowing us to walk in mental freedom. We acknowledge none of this would have been possible without your lead. You have provided strength in areas we once experienced the strongest levels of weakness. Having You by our side throughout this journey has been one of the greatest benefits. Your power pushed us over hurdles that were designed to trip us throughout the duration of our life. You provided us feet that carry the characteristics of hinds in order to overcome challenges placed before us. Our mental state is better because of You. We are much stronger because of You. Our gratitude will forever be the fruit of our lips. We honor You for who You are, and for what You have done. To You be all glory, honor, and gratitude. Praise and adoration belongs to You. Thank You for never leaving us alone in this process. It is our vow to You to remain free as we continue to press toward the mark of the high calling in Christ Jesus. Amen

Daily Affirmations

I carry the power to think my way through it. The ability to press my way to it and the faith to believe I can. Nothing will consume the freedom I have mentally fought for. My steps have been ordered to a path that provides peace and prosperity. I will continue to follow them with the help of the Holy Spirit as my guide.

Distractions no longer have the power to detour me; nor will thoughts have the strength to overtake me. God has granted me the authority to command mental alignment. I take charge over every thought that tries to come against His plan for my life.

My mind is no longer the devil's workshop. His attempt to control me has been cancelled by the power of God within. My thoughts are those that remain pleasing to Him. I give God full access to lead me in my everyday thinking. I will no longer think I am not who He says I am.

 My past does not define me, neither does it have the power to destroy me. Every hard thing shall be a brick toward the build of my betterment. Mentally I have overcome. Spiritually I have conquered. There is no thought that will cause me to believe differently.

Every negative thought that tries to rise against the peace of God granted to me has been canceled before it has the power to root itself where it no longer belongs. All mental weight has been replaced with the word of God that provides wisdom to guide me in better thinking. I stand on the manual my Father provided as a portrait of knowledge proven through the Holy Bible.

I won't mentally move from the guide given to me. My feet shall remain planted on His promises concerning my life. I shall be guided by the Spirit for where the Spirit of God is; there is liberty.

I choose peace over pain. There is nothing more important than the mental freedom I have gained. Every form of condemnation has been broken off of my mind. What happened to me did not change what God continuously think of me. Therefore, I will no longer spend time trying to alter His thoughts.

I am who He says I am. I will do what God has created me to do. I mentally believe He has the ability to use me in any capacity He so chooses. No longer will I tie His hands in executing the pre-ordained plan for my life. My mind is submitted to God. To Him I put all of my trust.

The hardest mental challenge is behind me. Nothing in my past has the ability to lead me down the journey of mental destruction. Mental clutter has been uprooted and dealt with. I take authority over all things negative that try to attach itself to my mind, my heart, and my spirit. Freedom will remain my abundant portion.

Mental clarity is my new way of thinking. I continue to press toward the mark of the high calling before me. I will obtain the goodness of God as I trust the path assigned to the remainder of my days. Goodness and mercy shall follow me as I continue to honor Christ forever.

About the Author

Nikilya Brown McNeil, affectionately known as "Niki", is the mother of three: Gabriel, Niya, and Isaiah. She is a 1996 graduate of Minor High School and is currently pursuing her degree in Business Management. Niki serves on the ministerial team of *The Purpose Church* under the leadership of Pastor Andrea and Elder Anthony Gates. Niki also serves as the Executive Director of God's Daughters, a nonprofit organization committed to ministering to women and young-age girls. To encounter her is to find her busy encouraging others and serving in any capacity needed. Her transparency can be felt by those who have been afforded the opportunity to hear her share her life experiences. Niki has an undying love for people with a strong desire to see them become the greatest they're afforded the opportunity to become.